EASY SI COOKBOOK

THE EFFORTLESS CHEF SERIES

By
Chef Maggie Chow
Copyright © 2015 by Saxonberg Associates
All rights reserved

Published by
BookSumo, a division of Saxonberg Associates
http://www.booksumo.com/

A Gift From Me To You...

[Send the Book!](#)

I know you like easy cooking. But what about Japanese Sushi?

Join my private reader's club and get a copy of ***Infinite Sushi: A Complete Set of Sushi and Japanese Recipes*** by fellow BookSumo author Hashimoto Kazuma for FREE!

Send the Book!

Enjoy some of the best sushi available!

You will also receive updates about all my new books when they are free. So please show your support.

Also don't forget to like and subscribe on the social networks. I love meeting my readers. Links to all my profiles are below so please click and connect :)

Facebook

Twitter

ABOUT THE AUTHOR.

Maggie Chow is the author and creator of your favorite *Easy Cookbooks* and *The Effortless Chef Series*. Maggie is a lover of all things related to food. Maggie loves nothing more than finding new recipes, trying them out, and then making them her own, by adding or removing ingredients, tweaking cooking times, and anything to make the recipe not only taste better, but be easier to cook!

For a complete listing of all my books please see my author page.

Introduction

Welcome to *The Effortless Chef Series*! Thank you for taking the time to download the *Easy Spinach Cookbook*. Come take a journey with me into the delights of easy cooking. The point of this cookbook and all my cookbooks is to exemplify the effortless nature of cooking simply.

In this book we focus on cooking with spinach. You will find that even though the recipes are simple, the taste of the dishes is quite amazing.

So will you join me in an adventure of simple cooking? If the answer is yes (and I hope it is) please consult the table of contents to find the dishes you are most interested in. Once you are ready jump right in and start cooking.

— Chef Maggie Chow

TABLE OF CONTENTS

A Gift From Me To You… 2
About the Author. 4
Introduction 6
Table of Contents 7
Any Issues? Contact Me 10
Legal Notes...11
Common Abbreviations........................12
Chapter 1: Easy Spinach Recipes 13
   Almond Salad 13
   Sweet and Savory Spinach Salad 16
   Mushroom Salad 19
   Kale and Spinach with Peppers and Balsamic..22
   Spinach Salad I 25
   Lentils for Autumn...........................27

Rustic Soup of Spinach.....................30

Asian Style Spinach Soup 33

Leeks and Spinach with Cannellini over Couscous 36

Easy Creamy Soup 39

Spinach and Curry 42

Spicy Chicken.....................................45

Artisan Soup of Artichokes and Mozzarella..48

Chicken Alfredo.................................51

Creamy Tortellini..............................54

Enhanced Chicken Breasts with Peppers...57

The Best Turkey Burgers 60

Maggie's Pasta Bake 63

Easy Pesto 66

West Indian Style Salad....................69

Maggie's Easy Calzones 72

Spinach Bites.....................................75

Orzo and Spinach..............................78

Soup of Ginger and Rice Noodles.....81

Ramen Salad......................................84
A Gift From Me To You.......................87
Come On...89
Let's Be Friends :) 89
Can I Ask A Favour? 90
Interested in Other Easy Cookbooks?..91

ANY ISSUES? CONTACT ME

If you find that something important to you is missing from this book please contact me at maggie@booksumo.com.

I will try my best to re-publish a revised copy taking your feedback into consideration and let you know when the book has been revised with you in mind.

:)

— Chef Maggie Chow

LEGAL NOTES

ALL RIGHTS RESERVED. NO PART OF THIS BOOK MAY BE REPRODUCED OR TRANSMITTED IN ANY FORM OR BY ANY MEANS. PHOTOCOPYING, POSTING ONLINE, AND / OR DIGITAL COPYING IS STRICTLY PROHIBITED UNLESS WRITTEN PERMISSION IS GRANTED BY THE BOOK'S PUBLISHING COMPANY. LIMITED USE OF THE BOOK'S TEXT IS PERMITTED FOR USE IN REVIEWS WRITTEN FOR THE PUBLIC AND/OR PUBLIC DOMAIN.

COMMON ABBREVIATIONS

cup(s)	C.
tablespoon	tbsp
teaspoon	tsp
ounce	oz.
pound	lb

*All units used are standard American measurements

Chapter 1: Easy Spinach Recipes

Almond Salad

Ingredients

- 8 C. chopped fresh spinach
- 2 tbsps canola oil
- 1 tbsp sesame oil
- 3 tbsps red wine vinegar
- 2 tsps Dijon mustard
- 1 tbsp honey
- 1 tsp salt
- 1/4 red onion, very thinly sliced
- 2 hard-boiled eggs, chopped
- 1/2 C. sliced toasted almonds
- ground black pepper to taste

Directions

- Get a big bowl to put all your spinach in.
- Boil: salt, sesame and canola oil, honey, vinegar, and mustard.
- Once everything is boiling coat your spinach with it.
- Let the leaves wilt down a bit.
- Now stir fry your onions in the same pan.
- Top the salad with: hard boiled eggs, black pepper, almonds, and onions.
- Enjoy.

Amount per serving (4 total)

Timing Information:

Preparation	Cooking	Total Time
20 m	10 m	30 m

Nutritional Information:

Calories	238 kcal
Fat	19.3 g
Carbohydrates	11.3g
Protein	7.5 g
Cholesterol	106 mg
Sodium	723 mg

* Percent Daily Values are based on a 2,000 calorie diet.

Sweet and Savory Spinach Salad

Ingredients

- 2 tbsps sesame seeds
- 1 tbsp poppy seeds
- 1/2 C. white sugar
- 1/2 C. olive oil
- 1/4 C. distilled white vinegar
- 1/4 tsp paprika
- 1/4 tsp Worcestershire sauce
- 1 tbsp minced onion
- 10 oz. fresh spinach - rinsed, dried and torn into bite-size pieces
- 1 quart strawberries - cleaned, hulled and sliced
- 1/4 C. almonds, blanched and slivered

Directions

- Get a bowl, combine: onions, sesame seeds, Worcestershire, poppy seeds, paprika, sugar, vinegar, and olive oil.
- Place some plastic wrap around the bowl and put everything in the fridge for 2 hrs.
- Get a 2nd bowl, mix: almonds, strawberries, and spinach.
- Combine both bowls and toss the leaves to coat everything evenly with sauce.
- Place the salad in the fridge for 20 mins.
- Enjoy.

Amount per serving (4 total)

Timing Information:

Preparation	Cooking	Total Time
10 m		1 h 10 m

Nutritional Information:

Calories	491 kcal
Fat	35.2 g
Carbohydrates	42.9g
Protein	6 g
Cholesterol	0 mg
Sodium	63 mg

* Percent Daily Values are based on a 2,000 calorie diet.

Mushroom Salad

Ingredients

- 4 slices bacon
- 2 eggs
- 2 tsps white sugar
- 2 tbsps cider vinegar
- 2 tbsps water
- 1/2 tsp salt
- 1 lb spinach
- 1/4 lb fresh mushrooms, sliced

Directions

- Fry your bacon and then break it into pieces. Set 2 tbsps of drippings aside for later.
- Boil water in a large pot and then once it is boiling add in your eggs.
- Continue boiling for 2 mins, with a lid on the pot, and then shut the heat.

- Let the eggs sit in the hot water for 10 to 15 mins. Now drain the liquid, remove the shells, and cut the eggs into wedges.
- Add your bacon drippings to a frying pan and then warm the following in it: salt, sugar, water, and vinegar.
- Cut the stems from your spinach and wash the leaves before placing them in a bowl.
- Toss the leaves with the wet mixture of vinegar and sugar. Toss the leave then garnish the salad with the eggs, mushrooms, and bacon.
- Enjoy.

Amount per serving (4 total)

Timing Information:

Preparation	Cooking	Total Time
15 m	30 m	45 m

Nutritional Information:

Calories	126 kcal
Fat	6.8 g
Carbohydrates	7.5g
Protein	10.6 g
Cholesterol	103 mg
Sodium	625 mg

* Percent Daily Values are based on a 2,000 calorie diet.

Kale and Spinach with Peppers and Balsamic

Ingredients

Salad:

- 1/2 bunch kale - stems removed and discarded, leaves torn into bite-size pieces
- 1/2 bunch fresh spinach, torn
- 1/2 head romaine lettuce, torn
- 1 large carrot, diced
- 1 large cucumber, diced
- 1/2 red bell pepper, diced

Dressing:

- 1/2 C. balsamic vinegar
- 1/2 C. extra-virgin olive oil
- 1 tbsp lemon juice
- 1 pinch sea salt
- 1 pinch ground black pepper

- 1 pinch garlic powder
- 1 pinch lemon pepper

Directions

- Get a bowl, mix: bell peppers, kale, cucumbers, spinach, carrots, and lettuce.
- Get a 2nd bowl, combine: lemon pepper, vinegar, garlic powder, olive oil, pepper, lemon juice, and sea salt.
- Combine both bowls. Toss the leaves to coat them evenly.
- Enjoy.

Amount per serving (6 total)

Timing Information:

Preparation	Cooking	Total Time
20 m		20 m

Nutritional Information:

Calories	228 kcal
Fat	19.3 g
Carbohydrates	12.7g
Protein	3 g
Cholesterol	0 mg
Sodium	147 mg

* Percent Daily Values are based on a 2,000 calorie diet.

Spinach Salad I

Ingredients

- 1 (6 ounce) package baby spinach leaves
- 1/3 C. cubed Cheddar cheese
- 1 Fuji apple - peeled, cored and diced
- 1/3 C. finely chopped red onion
- 1/4 C. sweetened dried cranberries
- 1/3 C. blanched slivered almonds
- 3 tbsps poppy seed salad dressing

Directions

- Get a bowl, toss: almonds, spinach, dressing, cranberries, cheddar, onions, and apples.
- Place the salad in the fridge for at least 20 to 30 mins.
- Enjoy.

Amount per serving (6 total)

Timing Information:

Preparation	Cooking	Total Time
15 m		15 m

Nutritional Information:

Calories	138 kcal
Fat	8.3 g
Carbohydrates	12.5g
Protein	3.8 g
Cholesterol	9 mg
Sodium	112 mg

* Percent Daily Values are based on a 2,000 calorie diet.

Lentils for Autumn

Ingredients

- 1/3 C. uncooked white rice
- 2/3 C. water
- 1 tsp vegetable oil
- 4 oz. turkey kielbasa, chopped
- 1 onion, minced
- 1 carrot, chopped
- 1/2 tsp crushed red pepper flakes
- 6 C. water
- 2 C. reduced sodium chicken broth
- 1 C. dry lentils
- 1 (10 ounce) bag fresh spinach, torn

Directions

- Boil your water and then add in your rice.

- Place a lid on the pot, and set the heat to low, before letting the contents simmer for 22 mins.
- Simultaneously stir fry your kielbasa until browned and then add in your carrots, onions, and red peppers.
- Stir fry everything until it is all soft.
- Now add the lentils and broth.
- Get the broth boiling, set the heat to low, and let the lentils lightly simmer for 27 mins.
- Combine the rice with the lentils and the spinach.
- Now cook the soup for 7 more mins.
- Enjoy warm.

Amount per serving (8 total)

Timing Information:

Preparation	Cooking	Total Time
15 m	35 m	50 m

Nutritional Information:

Calories	150 kcal
Fat	2.4 g
Carbohydrates	22.7g
Protein	10.1 g
Cholesterol	10 mg
Sodium	190 mg

* Percent Daily Values are based on a 2,000 calorie diet.

Rustic Soup of Spinach

Ingredients

- 1 lb frozen chopped spinach, thawed
- 2 C. water
- 4 tsps chicken bouillon granules
- 1/2 C. chopped onion
- 1/4 tsp garlic powder
- 1/4 C. butter
- 1/4 C. all-purpose flour
- 3 C. half-and-half
- salt and pepper to taste

Directions

- Boil the following, until your onions are soft: onions, garlic powder, water, spinach, and bouillon.
- Simultaneously form a roux by stirring flour slowly into melted butter.

- Cook this for 2 to 3 mins. Then add in your half and half and continue stirring.
- Combine this with the bouillon.
- Let the soup simmer for 12 more mins. Then add in your preferred amount of pepper and salt.
- Enjoy warm.

Amount per serving (5 total)

Timing Information:

Preparation	Cooking	Total Time
10 m	35 m	45 m

Nutritional Information:

Calories	330 kcal
Fat	26.7 g
Carbohydrates	16.7g
Protein	8.8 g
Cholesterol	78 mg
Sodium	609 mg

* Percent Daily Values are based on a 2,000 calorie diet.

ASIAN STYLE SPINACH SOUP

Ingredients

- 2 tbsps olive oil
- 1 onion, chopped
- 1 carrot, sliced
- 2 stalks celery, sliced
- 6 C. chicken stock
- 1/3 C. uncooked white rice
- 1 1/3 C. fresh spinach, washed and chopped
- 1 1/3 C. butter lettuce - rinsed, and torn into small pieces
- 1 1/3 C. chopped fresh parsley
- salt to taste
- ground black pepper to taste
- 1 pinch cayenne pepper

Directions

- Stir fry your onions, celery, and carrots until soft for 7 mins.

Combine in the chicken stock and get it boiling.
- Once everything is boiling pour in the rice, place a lid on the pot, set the heat to a low level, and let the rice cook for 22 to 35 mins until soft.
- Add in your parsley, lettuce and spinach and let the contents cook until soft for 3 mins. Now add the cayenne, pepper, and salt.
- Now take the contents out of the pan and blend it in batches. To make this process easier try using an immersion blender.
- Enjoy.

Amount per serving (7 total)

Timing Information:

Preparation	Cooking	Total Time
25 m	45 m	1 d 1 h 10

Nutritional Information:

Calories	103 kcal
Fat	4.7 g
Carbohydrates	13.9g
Protein	2.3 g
Cholesterol	1 mg
Sodium	685 mg

* Percent Daily Values are based on a 2,000 calorie diet.

Leeks and Spinach with Cannellini over Couscous

Ingredients

- 2 tsps olive oil
- 4 leeks, bulb only, chopped
- 2 cloves garlic, chopped
- 2 (16 ounce) cans fat-free chicken broth
- 2 (16 ounce) cans cannellini beans, rinsed and drained
- 2 bay leaves
- 2 tsps ground cumin
- 1/2 C. whole wheat couscous
- 2 C. packed fresh spinach
- salt and pepper to taste

Directions

- Fry your leeks in oil and garlic for 7 mins. Then add in your broth, cumin, bay leaves, and beans.

- Get the contents boiling and then add in your couscous.
- Place a lid on the pan and lower the heat.
- Let the couscous cook for 7 mins. Add in the pepper and salt and finally the spinach.
- Enjoy hot.

Amount per serving (8 total)

Timing Information:

Preparation	Cooking	Total Time
10 m	15 m	25 m

Nutritional Information:

Calories	179 kcal
Fat	2 g
Carbohydrates	30.6g
Protein	9.4 g
Cholesterol	0 mg
Sodium	432 mg

* Percent Daily Values are based on a 2,000 calorie diet.

EASY CREAMY SOUP

Ingredients

- 1 1/2 C. water
- 3 cubes chicken bouillon
- 1 (10 ounce) package frozen chopped spinach
- 3 tbsps butter
- 1/4 C. all-purpose flour
- 3 C. milk
- 1 tbsp dried minced onion
- salt and pepper to taste

Directions

- Boil the following in a large pot: spinach, bouillon, and water. Continue boiling until the spinach is soft.
- Get a 2nd large pot and stir the following, while heating, for 3 mins: butter, flour, and milk. Add the following seasons and stir for

half a sec: pepper, salt, and minced onions.
- Finally add in your spinach mix.
- Enjoy warm.

Amount per serving (4 total)

Timing Information:

Preparation	Cooking	Total Time
5 m	20 m	25 m

Nutritional Information:

Calories	227 kcal
Fat	12.9 g
Carbohydrates	19.1g
Protein	10.1 g
Cholesterol	38 mg
Sodium	1053 mg

* Percent Daily Values are based on a 2,000 calorie diet.

SPINACH AND CURRY

Ingredients

- 1 large potato - peeled and cubed
- 6 tbsps olive oil
- 1/2 C. chopped green onions
- 12 C. spinach - rinsed, stemmed, and dried
- 1/3 C. all-purpose flour
- 2 tsps curry powder
- 4 C. chicken broth
- 1 tbsp lemon juice
- 1 (8 ounce) carton nonfat sour cream

Directions

- Boil your potatoes until soft in water. Then remove all the liquid and place everything to the side.
- Fry your green onions until soft in 2 tbsps of olive oil. Then add the potatoes and the spinach.

- Cook the mix until everything is soft.
- Now process the mix in a blender until thick and smooth.
- Add more olive to a pan and combine curry and flour in it.
- Slowly add in the broth and keep stirring.
- Now add in the blended spinach and some lemon juice.
- Get the contents boiling and keep stirring.
- Get a bowl and add in some sour cream.
- Top the cream with 1 C. of soup and stir the contents until smooth.
- Add this mix back into the large pot and heat everything for 2 more mins.
- Enjoy hot.

Amount per serving (8 total)

Timing Information:

Preparation	Cooking	Total Time
15 m	20 m	35 m

Nutritional Information:

Calories	181 kcal
Fat	10.5 g
Carbohydrates	18.1g
Protein	4.7 g
Cholesterol	4 mg
Sodium	84 mg

* Percent Daily Values are based on a 2,000 calorie diet.

SPICY CHICKEN

Ingredients

- 1 (10 ounce) package fresh spinach leaves
- 1/2 C. sour cream
- 1/2 C. shredded pepper jack cheese
- 4 cloves garlic, minced
- 4 skinless, boneless chicken breast halves - flattened to 1/2 inch thickness
- 1 pinch ground black pepper
- 8 slices bacon

Directions

- Set the oven to 375 degrees before doing anything else.
- Get a bowl and put your spinach in it. Cook everything for 4 mins in the microwave.

- Now add in the garlic, pepper jack, and sour cream. Stir the contents.
- Evenly divide the spinach mix between your chicken breasts and place the mix in the center of each. Now roll your chicken.
- Take 2 pieces of bacon and wrap them around the chicken rolls and stake a toothpick between each roll to help hold its shape.
- Place everything in a casserole dish and cook for 35 mins in the oven at 375 degrees.
- Finish the cooking for 7 mins at 500 degrees.
- Enjoy.

Amount per serving (4 total)

Timing Information:

Preparation	Cooking	Total Time
15 m	45 m	1 h

Nutritional Information:

Calories	356 kcal
Fat	20.5 g
Carbohydrates	5.7g
Protein	36.5 g
Cholesterol	113 mg
Sodium	565 mg

* Percent Daily Values are based on a 2,000 calorie diet.

Artisan Soup of Artichokes and Mozzarella

Ingredients

- 1 (8 ounce) package cream cheese, softened
- 1/4 C. mayonnaise
- 1/4 C. grated Parmesan cheese
- 1/4 C. grated Romano cheese
- 1 clove garlic, peeled and minced
- 1/2 tsp dried basil
- 1/4 tsp garlic salt
- salt and pepper to taste
- 1 (14 ounce) can artichoke hearts, drained and chopped
- 1/2 C. frozen chopped spinach, thawed and drained
- 1/4 C. shredded mozzarella cheese

Directions

- Coat a casserole dish with oil and then set your oven to 350 degrees before doing anything else.
- Get a bowl, combine: pepper, cream cheese, salt, mayo, garlic salt, parmesan, basil, Romano, and garlic.
- Add in your spinach and artichoke hearts.
- Place all the contents in the casserole dish and garnish everything with mozzarella.
- Cook everything in the oven for 25 to 30 mins.
- Enjoy.

Amount per serving (12 total)

Timing Information:

Preparation	Cooking	Total Time
15 m	25 m	40 m

Nutritional Information:

Calories	134 kcal
Fat	11.7 g
Carbohydrates	3.4g
Protein	4.4 g
Cholesterol	28 mg
Sodium	315 mg

* Percent Daily Values are based on a 2,000 calorie diet.

CHICKEN ALFREDO

Ingredients

- 2 tbsps olive oil
- 2 cloves garlic, finely chopped
- 4 skinless, boneless chicken breast halves - cut into strips
- 2 C. fresh spinach leaves
- 1 (4.5 ouncc) package dry Alfredo sauce mix
- 2 tbsps pesto
- 1 (8 ounce) package dry penne pasta
- 1 tbsp grated Romano cheese

Directions

- Boil your pasta for 7 mins in water and salt. Then remove all liquids.
- Stir fry your garlic for 2 mins and then combine your chicken with

it and cook the chicken for 9 more mins per side.
- Now add in the spinach and stir fry everything for 5 mins.
- Heat your Alfredo sauce simultaneously.
- Once it is hot spoon in two 2 tbsps of pesto and shut the heat.
- Combine the chicken with the pasta and top everything with the Alfredo sauce.
- Finally add a garnishing of cheese.
- Enjoy.

Amount per serving (4 total)

Timing Information:

Preparation	Cooking	Total Time
20 m	35 m	55 m

Nutritional Information:

Calories	572 kcal
Fat	19.3 g
Carbohydrates	57.3g
Protein	41.9 g
Cholesterol	84 mg
Sodium	1707 mg

* Percent Daily Values are based on a 2,000 calorie diet.

CREAMY TORTELLINI

Ingredients

- 1 (16 ounce) package cheese tortellini
- 1 (14.5 ounce) can diced tomatoes with garlic and onion
- 1 C. chopped fresh spinach
- 1/2 tsp salt
- 1/4 tsp pepper
- 1 1/2 tsps dried basil
- 1 tsp minced garlic
- 2 tbsps all-purpose flour
- 3/4 C. milk
- 3/4 C. heavy cream
- 1/4 C. grated Parmesan cheese

Directions

- Boil your pasta for 12 mins. The remove all the liquid.

- Simultaneously stir fry until bubbling: garlic, tomatoes, basil, spinach, pepper, and salt.
- Get a bowl, mix, until smooth: cream, milk, and flour. Add this mix to the tomatoes and add the parmesan as well.
- Combine the pasta with the sauce and stir.
- Enjoy.

Amount per serving (6 total)

Timing Information:

Preparation	Cooking	Total Time
20 m	20 m	40 m

Nutritional Information:

Calories	400 kcal
Fat	19.7 g
Carbohydrates	43.9g
Protein	14.8 g
Cholesterol	79 mg
Sodium	885 mg

* Percent Daily Values are based on a 2,000 calorie diet.

Enhanced Chicken Breasts with Peppers

Ingredients

- 1/3 C. grated Parmesan cheese
- 1/4 tsp Italian seasoning
- 6 skinless, boneless chicken breasts
- 1/4 C. chopped green onions
- 1 tbsp butter
- 1 tbsp all-purpose flour
- 1/2 C. skim milk
- 1/2 (10 ounce) package frozen chopped spinach, thawed and drained
- 1 tbsp chopped pimento peppers

Directions

- Set your oven to 350 degrees before doing anything else.
- Season your chicken with the cheese and Italian seasoning by

placing everything in a bowl. Place the chicken pieces in a casserole dish.
- Stir fry your onions in butter and add in milk and flour. Continue heating and stirring for 2 mins or until the contents are lightly boiling.
- Add in the spinach and pimiento and let the spinach wilt.
- Cover your chicken first with the remaining seasonings and then with the spinach mix.
- Cook the chicken in the oven for 37 to 40 mins.
- Enjoy.

Amount per serving (6 total)

Timing Information:

Preparation	Cooking	Total Time
10 m	35 m	45 m

Nutritional Information:

Calories	186 kcal
Fat	4.8 g
Carbohydrates	3.6g
Protein	30.8 g
Cholesterol	78 mg
Sodium	185 mg

* Percent Daily Values are based on a 2,000 calorie diet.

THE BEST TURKEY BURGERS

Ingredients

- 2 eggs, beaten
- 2 cloves garlic, minced
- 4 oz. feta cheese
- 1 (10 ounce) box frozen chopped spinach, thawed and squeezed dry
- 2 lbs ground turkey

Directions

- Oil your grilling grate on a grill and get everything hot.
- Get a bowl, mix: turkey, eggs, spinach, feta, and garlic.
- Make at least 8 patties from this.
- Grill these patties in batches for 17 to 22 mins.
- Enjoy.

NOTE: You can also pan fry these patties or bake them in the oven until you find that the turkey is cooked through. But the best taste will be achieved with an outdoor grill.

Amount per serving (8 total)

Timing Information:

Preparation	Cooking	Total Time
20 m	15 m	35 m

Nutritional Information:

Calories	234 kcal
Fat	13 g
Carbohydrates	2.4g
Protein	27.4 g
Cholesterol	143 mg
Sodium	266 mg

* Percent Daily Values are based on a 2,000 calorie diet.

MAGGIE'S PASTA BAKE

Ingredients

- 1 (12 ounce) package medium seashell pasta
- 1 (10 ounce) package frozen chopped spinach, thawed
- 2 eggs
- 1/4 C. olive oil
- 1/2 C. bread crumbs
- 1 1/2 (26 ounce) jars tomato basil pasta sauce
- 1 (8 ounce) package shredded Cheddar cheese
- 1 (8 ounce) package shredded mozzarella cheese

Directions

- Set your oven to 350 degrees before doing anything else.
- Boil your pasta for 7 mins in water and salt. Then remove all

the liquid. Place the pasta in a bowl.
- Cook your spinach in 1.5 C. of boiling water in the same pot.
- Get a 2nd bowl, mix: oil and eggs.
- Combine the oil and eggs with the pasta and also some bread crumbs.
- Toss everything.
- In a casserole dish pour 1/3 of your pasta sauce, half of the pasta, 1/3 more of sauce, and then half the mozzarella and cheddar.
- Continue layering in this manner until all ingredients have been used completely.
- Cook the casserole in the oven for 50 mins.
- Let the casserole sit for 10 mins before eating.
- Enjoy.

Amount per serving (12 total)

Timing Information:

Preparation	Cooking	Total Time
15 m	1 h	1 h 15 m

Nutritional Information:

Calories	378 kcal
Fat	18 g
Carbohydrates	38g
Protein	17 g
Cholesterol	64 mg
Sodium	668 mg

* Percent Daily Values are based on a 2,000 calorie diet.

EASY PESTO

Ingredients

- 1 1/2 C. baby spinach leaves
- 3/4 C. fresh basil leaves
- 1/2 C. toasted pine nuts
- 1/2 C. grated Parmesan cheese
- 4 cloves garlic, peeled and quartered
- 3/4 tsp kosher salt
- 1/2 tsp freshly ground black pepper
- 1 tbsp fresh lemon juice
- 1/2 tsp lemon zest
- 1/2 C. extra-virgin olive oil

Directions

- Get a blender or food processor and blend the following: 2 tbsps of olive oil, spinach, lemon zest, basil, lemon juice, pine nuts,

pepper, parmesan, salt, and garlic.
- Add the rest of the oil and blend a few more times.
- Enjoy over cooked pasta.

Amount per serving (24 total)

Timing Information:

Preparation	Cooking	Total Time
20 m		20 m

Nutritional Information:

Calories	67 kcal
Fat	6.6 g
Carbohydrates	0.8g
Protein	1.5 g
Cholesterol	1 mg
Sodium	87 mg

* Percent Daily Values are based on a 2,000 calorie diet.

WEST INDIAN STYLE SALAD

Ingredients

- 6 eggs
- 1/2 lb bacon
- 2 lbs spinach, rinsed and chopped
- 2 3/4 oz. croutons
- 1/4 C. sliced fresh mushrooms
- 1 onion, chopped
- 2/3 C. white sugar
- 1 tsp salt
- 1 C. vegetable oil
- 1/3 C. cider vinegar
- 1/2 tsp ground black pepper
- 1 tsp celery seed
- 1 tbsp prepared Dijon-style mustard

Directions

- Add some water to a large pot and get it boiling.
- Once it is boiling, add your eggs.

- Place a lid on the pot and shut the heat.
- Let the eggs sit in the water for 14 mins. Then remove the shells and dice the eggs.
- Fry your bacon and once it is crispy break it into pieces.
- Blend or process the following in a blender or food processor until smooth: mustard, onions, celery seed, sugar, pepper, salt, pepper, oil, and vinegar. This is your dressing.
- Get a bowl, combine: mushrooms, eggs, croutons, bacon, and spinach together.
- Add your dressing to the bowl and toss the contents to coat all the leaves evenly.
- Enjoy.

Amount per serving (8 total)

Timing Information:

Preparation	Cooking	Total Time
15 m	15 m	30 m

Nutritional Information:

Calories	483 kcal
Fat	37.3 g
Carbohydrates	27g
Protein	12.4 g
Cholesterol	150 mg
Sodium	774 mg

* Percent Daily Values are based on a 2,000 calorie diet.

Maggie's Easy Calzones

Ingredients

- 1 (15 ounce) container ricotta cheese
- 2 eggs
- 2 tbsps dried Italian seasoning
- 3 C. shredded mozzarella cheese
- 1 C. freshly grated Parmesan cheese
- 1 (10 ounce) package frozen chopped spinach, thawed and squeezed dry
- salt and pepper to taste
- 1 (32 ounce) package frozen white bread dough, thawed

Directions

- Set your oven to 450 degrees before doing anything else.

- Get a bowl, combine evenly: spinach, ricotta, mozzarella, eggs, Italian seasoning, and parmesan.
- Break your dough into 8 even pieces and flatten each piece into a circle that is at least 8 inches in diameter.
- Evenly divide your cheese mix between each piece of dough.
- Fold your dough to form a semi-circle and press the edges with a fork.
- Layer each piece on a baking sheet or in a casserole dish that has been oiled or coated with nonstick spray.
- Cook everything in the oven for 35 mins.
- Enjoy.

Amount per serving (8 total)

Timing Information:

Preparation	Cooking	Total Time
1 h	30 m	1 h 30 m

Nutritional Information:

Calories	584 kcal
Fat	20.6 g
Carbohydrates	61.2g
Protein	35.5 g
Cholesterol	101 mg
Sodium	1200 mg

* Percent Daily Values are based on a 2,000 calorie diet.

SPINACH BITES

Ingredients

- 2 (10 ounce) packages frozen chopped spinach, thawed and drained
- 2 C. Italian-style seasoned bread crumbs
- 1 C. grated Parmesan cheese
- 1/2 C. butter, melted
- 4 small green onion, finely chopped
- 4 eggs, lightly beaten
- salt and pepper to taste

Directions

- Set your oven to 350 degrees before doing anything else.
- Get a bowl, combine: pepper, spinach, salt, eggs, butter, bread crumbs, green onions, and parmesan.

- Form as many little balls as you can from this mix.
- Try to shape them evenly so that each one is about one inch in size.
- Bake these spinach balls in the oven for 14 mins.
- Enjoy as an appetizer or side dish.

Amount per serving (10 total)

Timing Information:

Preparation	Cooking	Total Time
15 m	15 m	30 m

Nutritional Information:

Calories	258 kcal
Fat	15.6 g
Carbohydrates	19.1g
Protein	11.8 g
Cholesterol	108 mg
Sodium	633 mg

* Percent Daily Values are based on a 2,000 calorie diet.

ORZO AND SPINACH

Ingredients

- 1 (16 ounce) package uncooked orzo
- 1/2 C. olive oil
- 2 tbsps butter
- 1/2 tsp minced garlic
- 1/2 tsp dried basil
- 1/2 tsp crushed red pepper flakes
- 1 C. pine nuts
- 1 (10 ounce) bag baby spinach
- 1/8 C. balsamic vinegar
- 1 (8 ounce) package crumbled feta cheese
- 1/2 fresh tomato, chopped
- salt to taste

Directions

- Boil your pasta for 9 mins in water and salt. Then remove all the liquids.

- Place everything in a bowl.
- Fry your pine nuts, garlic, red pepper, and basil in butter and olive oil for 3 mins. Then combine in the spinach, place a lid on the pot, and let the spinach cook down for 6 mins.
- Add the spinach mix to the pasta and toss everything. Then add some balsamic vinegar and toss again.
- Add your preferred amount of salt and pepper and then some feta, and tomatoes.
- Enjoy.

Amount per serving (8 total)

Timing Information:

Preparation	Cooking	Total Time
15 m	15 m	30 m

Nutritional Information:

Calories	550 kcal
Fat	32.5 g
Carbohydrates	49.1g
Protein	17.4 g
Cholesterol	33 mg
Sodium	514 mg

* Percent Daily Values are based on a 2,000 calorie diet.

Soup of Ginger and Rice Noodles

Ingredients

- 1 tbsp vegetable oil
- 2 tsps minced fresh garlic
- 2 tsps minced fresh ginger root
- 1 (10 ounce) package frozen chopped spinach, thawed and drained
- salt and black pepper to taste
- 2 quarts chicken stock
- 1 cup shrimp stock
- 1 tsp hot pepper sauce(optional)
- 1 tsp hoisin sauce(optional)
- 20 peeled and deveined medium shrimp
- 1 (6.75 ounce) package long rice noodles (rice vermicelli)
- 2 green onions, chopped(optional)

Directions

- Cook the garlic and ginger for about one minute before adding spinach, pepper, and salt.
- Cook this mix for 3 more minutes to get the spinach tender.
- Now add the chicken stock, hoisin sauce, shrimp stock and hot pepper sauce, and cook this for a 2 more mins.
- Finally add the noodles and shrimp.
- Cook for 4 minutes before adding green onions and cooking everything for five minutes.
- Add salt and pepper according to your tastes before serving.
- Enjoy.

Serving: 6

Timing Information:

Preparation	Cooking	Total Time
15 mins	20 mins	40 mins

Nutritional Information:

Calories	212 kcal
Carbohydrates	28.6 g
Cholesterol	52 mg
Fat	4.7 g
Fiber	2.7 g
Protein	14.4 g
Sodium	1156 mg

* Percent Daily Values are based on a 2,000 calorie diet.

Ramen Salad

Ingredients

- 2 (3 ounce) packages chicken flavored ramen noodles
- 8 cups torn spinach leaves
- 2 cups cooked and cubed chicken
- 1 cup seedless red grapes, halved
- 1 cup sliced red bell peppers
- 1/2 cup chopped cashews
- 1/2 cup Gorgonzola cheese, crumbled
- 4 cloves garlic, minced
- 1 lemon, juiced
- 1/3 cup olive oil
- 1/4 cup light mayonnaise
- 1 red bell pepper, sliced
- 20 grape clusters, for garnish

Directions

- Cook ramen noodles in boiling water for about 2 minutes and drain everything with the help of a colander.
- Mix torn spinach leaves, halved grapes, blue cheese, cooked

turkey or chicken, red pepper, cashews and ramen noodles very thoroughly in a large bowl.
- In another bowl; whisk lemon juice, flavor packets, oil, garlic and mayonnaise.
- Combine both bowls and add some rings of red pepper and small grape clusters.
- Serve.

Serving: 2

Timing Information:

Preparation	Cooking	Total Time
15 mins	10 mins	25 mins

Nutritional Information:

Calories	147 kcal
Carbohydrates	11 g
Cholesterol	17 mg
Fat	8.6 g
Fiber	1.3 g
Protein	7.2 g
Sodium	177 mg

* Percent Daily Values are based on a 2,000 calorie diet.

A Gift From Me To You...

[Send the Book!](#)

I know you like easy cooking. But what about Japanese Sushi?

Join my private reader's club and get a copy of ***Infinite Sushi: A Complete Set of Sushi and Japanese Recipes*** by fellow BookSumo author Hashimoto Kazuma for FREE!

Send the Book!

Enjoy some of the best sushi available!

You will also receive updates about all my new books when they are free. So please show your support.

Also don't forget to like and subscribe on the social networks. I love meeting my readers. Links to all my profiles are below so please click and connect :)

Facebook

Twitter

Come On...
Let's Be Friends :)

I adore my readers and love connecting with them socially. Please follow the links below so we can connect on Facebook, Twitter, and Google+.

Facebook

Twitter

I also have a blog that I regularly update for my readers so check it out below.

My Blog

CAN I ASK A FAVOUR?

If you found this book interesting, or have otherwise found any benefit in it. Then may I ask that you post a review of it on Amazon? Nothing excites me more than new reviews, especially reviews which suggest new topics for writing. I do read all reviews and I always factor feedback into my newer works.

So if you are willing to take ten minutes to write what you sincerely thought about this book then please visit our Amazon page and post your opinions.

Again thank you!

INTERESTED IN OTHER EASY COOKBOOKS?

Everything is easy! Check out my Amazon Author page for more great cookbooks:

For a complete listing of all my books please see my author page.

Printed in Germany
by Amazon Distribution
GmbH, Leipzig